AGES
6-8

Who's There?

70 Original **Knock Knock** Jokes For Kids

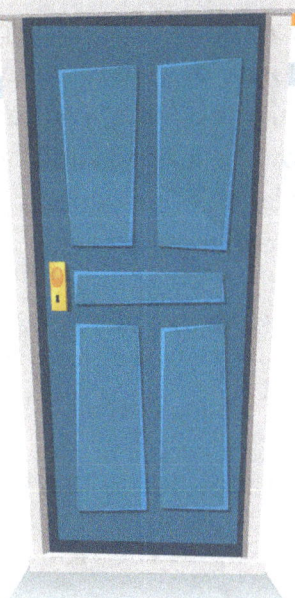

Two Little Ravens

CHILDREN'S NON-FICTION BOOKS

Paperback Edition: 9781960320360
Hardcover Edition: 9781960320377
Digital Edition: 9781960320384

Published in the United States by Two Ravens Books LLC,

254 Chapman Rd, Ste 209, Newark DE 19702

'Expand the mind, free the imagination, one title at a time.'
www.tworavensbooks.com

KNOCK KNOCK

WHO'S THERE?

Olive.

Olive who?

Olive you and I miss you!

KNOCK KNOCK

WHO'S THERE?

Harry.

Harry who?

Harry up and answer the door!

KNOCK KNOCK

WHO'S THERE?

Goat.

Goat who?

Goat to be kidding, you're great at these jokes!

WHO'S THERE?

Wooden shoe.

Wooden shoe who?

Wooden shoe like to hear another joke?

WHO'S THERE?

Banana.

Banana who?

**Banana split!
The ice cream is melting!**

KNOCK KNOCK

WHO'S THERE?

Tuna.

Tuna who?

Tuna in tomorrow for more great jokes!

WHO'S THERE?

Alaska.

Alaska who?

Alaska my mom if we can have ice cream!

KNOCK KNOCK

WHO'S THERE?

Police.

Police who?

Police stop telling these funny jokes!

KNOCK KNOCK

WHO'S THERE?

Olive.

Olive who?

Olive next door, remember?

WHO'S THERE?

Ears.

Ears who?

Ears another joke for you!

KNOCK
KNOCK

WHO'S THERE?

Ada.

Ada who?

Ada burger for lunch today!

KNOCK KNOCK

WHO'S THERE?

Justin.

Justin who?

Justin time for another joke!

WHO'S THERE?

Otto.

Otto who?

Otto know. I've forgotten my joke!

KNOCK KNOCK

WHO'S THERE?

Wade.

Wade who?

Wade a minute and I'll tell you!

KNOCK KNOCK

WHO'S THERE?

Yuri.

Yuri who?

Yuri member of this joke club too?

KNOCK KNOCK

WHO'S THERE?

Berry.

Berry who?

Berry glad to know you!

KNOCK KNOCK

WHO'S THERE?

Water.

Water who?

Water you waiting for? It's joke time!

KNOCK KNOCK

WHO'S THERE?

Jewel.

Jewel who?

Jewel be sorry if you miss the next joke!

WHO'S THERE?

Leaf.

Leaf who?

Leaf me alone, I'm telling jokes!

WHO'S THERE?

Olive.

Olive who?

Olive the jokes you tell!

WHO'S THERE?

Felix.

Felix who?

Felix like it's going to rain, better get inside!

KNOCK KNOCK

WHO'S THERE?

Nova.

Nova who?

Nova good joke when I hear one!

KNOCK KNOCK

WHO'S THERE?

Uno.

Uno who?

Uno, draw four! Got any more knock-knock jokes?

WHO'S THERE?

Doris.

Doris who?

Doris locked, that's why I had to knock!

WHO'S THERE?

Lettuce.

Lettuce who?

Lettuce in, we brought the jokes!

WHO'S THERE?

Lemon.

Lemon who?

Lemon know when you're ready for more jokes!

KNOCK KNOCK

WHO'S THERE?

Orange.

Orange who?

Orange you excited for another joke?

KNOCK
KNOCK

WHO'S THERE?

Harry.

Harry who?

Harry up and get ready
for the next joke!

KNOCK KNOCK

WHO'S THERE?

Ben.

Ben who?

Ben waiting to tell you this joke!

KNOCK KNOCK

WHO'S THERE?

Avery.

Avery who?

Avery minute without laughter is a minute wasted!

KNOCK KNOCK

WHO'S THERE?

Tara.

Tara who?

Tara-riffic day starts with a great joke!

KNOCK KNOCK

WHO'S THERE?

Wendy.

Wendy who?

Wendy wind blows, don't forget to laugh!

KNOCK KNOCK

WHO'S THERE?

Tiger.

Tiger who?

Tiger shoe, your laces are undone!

KNOCK KNOCK

WHO'S THERE?

Pasta.

Pasta who?

Pasta your bedtime!

WHO'S THERE?

Wooden shoe.

Wooden shoe who?

Wooden shoe like to know!

WHO'S THERE?

Orange.

Orange who?

Orange you going to laugh at this peel-arious joke?

WHO'S THERE?

Dot.

Dot who?

Dot's all for now, folks!

TWORAVENS
B O O K S

Collectible imprints
for little learners & readers

Xander & Rem
Children's Coloring & Activity Books

Xander's Perch
CHILDREN'S FICTION BOOKS

Two Little Ravens
CHILDREN'S NON-FICTION BOOKS

Hello Brilliant Little Explorer and Grown-Up Guide!

Thanks for embarking on the fun-filled educational journey in this book.

If you have ideas to make this book more helpful for you and others, don't hesitate to email us at **hello@ tworavensbooks.com.**

If your funny bone was tickled and your brain ignited by this adventure, we'd be delighted if you could share your giggles and gains by reviewing **Who's There?.**

Your feedback not only helps others find this book but also fuels us to keep weaving humor and knowledge into more wonderful titles.

Keep laughing, keep learning, and thank you for your support of **Two Little Ravens**, an imprint of **Two Ravens Books LLC.**

Find more humorously educational books like this at TwoRavensBooks.com